D1470112

Easy Appetizers

by Kim Upton and Bev Bennett

BARRON'S

Woodbury, New York · London · Toronto · Sydney

All inquiries should be addressed to:

Barron's Educational Series, Inc.
113 Crossways Park Drive
Woodbury, New York 11797

International Standard Book
No. 0-8120-5556-X
Library of Congress Catalog Card
No. 83-21393

**Library of Congress Cataloging
in Publication Data**
Upton, Kim.
  Easy appetizers.

  (Easy cooking)
  Includes index.
  1. Cookery (Appetizers) I. Bennett, Bev. II. Title.
III. Series.
TX740.U68 1984   641.8'12   83-21393
ISBN 0-8120-5556-X

PRINTED IN HONG KONG
  4 5 6   490   9 8 7 6 5 4 3 2 1

Credits

Photography
Color photographs: Irwin Horowitz
Food stylist: Helen Feingold
Stylist: Hal Walter

Authors Bev Bennett and Kim Upton are food
  writers for the Chicago *Sun-Times*

Cover and book design Milton Glaser, Inc.

Series editor Carole Berglie

INTRODUCTION

Say appetizers and you've said a mouthful.

They are the food for any occasion, from between-meal snacks to elaborate dinners. Appetizers can be quick and easy tidbits or sophisticated combinations to serve as a first course.

These tempting morsels come in myriad colors, shapes, and ingredients. The flavors range from refreshingly subtle to just this side of fiery.

This book has appetizer recipes and suggestions to fit every need and taste.

For those who enjoy beginning dinner with a lovely, cold first course, there is a delightful dish of cold pasta with spicy peanut sauce, or roasted peppers with olives and lime juice, or, as a third choice, tabbouleh in red cabbage cups.

For those who like it hot, there are equally appealing first courses that require little effort. Salmon strudel, blue cheese tartlets, and pastry puffs filled with savory cheese are the possibilities.

Appetizers aren't just a signal to start a meal, however. They can be an event in themselves.

Lovely little arrangements such as cherry tomatoes topped with basil mayonnaise, taramosalata in pea pods, curried chicken and papaya kabobs, and asparagus wrapped in smoked salmon won't tax a harried host or hostess.

Some cold appetizers—marinated mushrooms, sirloin teriyaki, and zesty shrimp, for example—actually improve in flavor if made a day in advance. Feta and dill dip, herbed garlic dip, and a marvelous tomato salsa with orange will sit in the refrigerator for a couple of days.

If you prefer an instant party menu in your freezer, prepare pecan pick-ups, whole-wheat pretzels, and cheese sticks. Wrap, date, and freeze them. They will stay fresh as long as six months

and thaw (unwrapped at room temperature) in about an hour.

While cold foods require less last-minute preparation than do hot ones, including both makes an enjoyable selection.

Samosas, Chinese pearl balls, curry-stuffed wontons, chicken drumettes, chicken triangles, grape leaves with goat cheese, and corn fritters with ginger syrup can all be made up to an hour in advance. They can be kept warm, reheated, or served tepid.

To keep warm, simply place the appetizers on a cookie sheet in an oven heated to the lowest temperature. The baked grape leaves, samosas, and pearl balls will stay warm for as long as thirty minutes if placed on a serving tray and covered with foil. But don't cover fried foods with foil or they will become soggy.

One of the party giver's great dilemmas is to estimate how much food to provide.

A sit-down dinner is portion controlled. Each person is served one appetizer.

However, there are no restraints at a cocktail party where guests arrive at varying times and with varying appetites. It's usually wise to overestimate how much people will eat at a party at which liquor is served.

Allow about seven or eight pieces of food per person. If there's a showpiece appetizer, make enough so that everyone gets a taste. Every recipe in the book can be doubled or tripled according to the guest list. In some cases special information is given.

Don't forget to offer bowls of cut-up fruits and vegetables. Dieters will appreciate the chance to satisfy their urge to nibble.

The art of arranging an appetizer assortment is easy to learn. Choose serving platters in colors that complement the foods. Blue is one of the most flattering colors food can be matched with. Garnishes of parsley bouquets, cherry tomatoes, and deep green lettuce also set food off nicely.

Don't overcrowd food on the serving platters. Arrange each item so it is easy to pick up. If forks or toothpicks are necessary, place them next to the platter.

Occasionally check the appetizer table to see if any platters need replenishing. Do so when the food is half to three-fourths gone, but hasn't completely vanished (unless you're giving your guests a gentle hint about the hour).

Here are some additional suggestions that need only a few minutes and a few ingredients:

- Wrap a slice of prosciutto around a kiwifruit wedge.

- Remove the pimientos from green olives and substitute smoked almonds.

- Fill a green or red bell pepper with an herbed cream cheese. Chill. Cut into rings and serve.

- Boil small new potatoes. Dry. Cut in half and scoop out the centers from each, leaving a ¼-inch shell. Fill cavities with sour cream and top with a good sprinkling of red or black caviar.

- Drain a can of garbanzo beans. Pat the beans dry and generously sprinkle with freshly ground black pepper. Set out in bowls as you would nuts.

- Cut an eggroll wrapper into quarters or four strips. Deep-fry until golden and serve with a commercially made sweet and sour sauce for dipping.

- For homemade trail mix combine ½ cup each of raisins and shredded coconut, and 1 cup each of raw cashews, raw sunflower seeds, and roasted peanuts.

- Cut corn tortillas in half. Sprinkle half of each half with shredded monterey jack cheese. Top with a sliver of canned chili. Fold over and place on a greased cookie sheet. Bake in preheated 350-degree oven five minutes or until cheese melts.

- Hollow out a round Italian bread. Brush insides with melted butter. Then broil in preheated broiler up to two minutes. Watch carefully; bread can burn easily. Fill with a cheese spread, liver pâté or commercially made liverwurst.

- Set out pretzel sticks with bowls of strong mustard for dipping.

- Scoop semi-soft processed cheese spread into small balls and roll in chopped pecans.

- Fry bacon strips until crisp but still pliable. Wrap around avocado slices that have been brushed with lemon juice.

- Thinly slice regular or sweet potatoes and deep-fry for homemade chips.

- Combine 8 ounces cream cheese, ¼ cup chopped walnuts, and honey to taste. Blend well until light and airy. Serve as a fruit dip.

- Prepare corn fritters without the vegetables. Dip well-drained artichoke hearts in the batter, then deep-fry.

UNDERSTANDING THE RECIPE ANALYSES

For each recipe in this book, you'll note that we have provided data on the quantities of protein, fat, sodium, carbohydrates, and potassium, as well as the number of calories (kcal) per serving. If you are on a low-calorie diet or are watching your intake of sodium, for example, these figures should help you gauge your eating habits and help you balance your meals. Bear in mind, however, that the calculations are fundamentally estimates and are to be followed only in a very general way. The actual quantity of fat, for example, that may be contained in a given portion will vary with the quality of meat you buy or with how much care you take in skimming off cooking fat. If you are on a rigid diet, consult your physician. The analyses are based on the number of portions given as the yield for the recipe, but if the yield reads, "4 to 6 servings," we indicate which number of servings (4, for example) was used to determine the final amounts.

YIELD

8 to 10 servings
(about 1¾ cups)

Per serving (9)
calories 219, protein 1 g,
fat 23 g, sodium 293 mg,
carbohydrates 2 g,
potassium 85 mg

TIME

15 minutes preparation

INGREDIENTS

3 ounces cream cheese
1 clove garlic
1 small onion
1 bunch fresh parsley
¼ teaspoon dried tarragon
3 tablespoons white wine vinegar
½ teaspoon salt
Several dashes white pepper
1 cup mayonnaise
Assorted fresh vegetables, washed
      and dried

About 30 minutes ahead, take cream cheese out of refrigerator to soften, or use a presoftened variety.

Peel and mince the garlic ①. Mince the onion and measure so you have 3 tablespoons ②. Chop the parsley ③ and measure; you should have about ¾ cup.

In a blender or food processor, mix all ingredients except mayonnaise and vegetables. Stir in mayonnaise and chill dip until ready to serve. Serve with crisp fresh vegetables.

YIELD

4 to 6 servings

Per serving (4)
calories 243, protein 6 g,
fat 5 g, sodium 148 mg,
carbohydrates 44 g,
potassium 177 mg

TIME

30 minutes preparation
3 minutes cooking

INGREDIENTS

¼ cup distilled white vinegar
¼ cup plus 2 tablespoons sugar
1¾ cups warm cooked rice
2½ ounces prosciutto or smoked ham,
    sliced ¹⁄₁₆ inch thick
¼ melon of choice or a similar
    amount of papaya or about 3
    tablespoons golden caviar
Soy sauce
Minced chives

Combine vinegar and sugar in a saucepan over low heat and bring to a boil, stirring constantly. When sugar is dissolved, remove from heat and add 3 tablespoons of it to warm rice. Stir and let sit for a few minutes so that rice has a chance to absorb liquid.

Spread a thin layer of sticky rice over prosciutto or ham slices ①. Cut melon into wedges ½ inch in diameter. Place a wedge of fruit or a sprinkling of caviar across short end of rice-covered prosciutto ② and roll up jellyroll fashion ③. Repeat with remaining ingredients.

Using a very sharp knife, slice rolls into ¾-inch-thick slices. Serve with a bowl of soy sauce sprinkled with minced fresh chives. Serve cold.

YIELD

6 to 8 servings

Per serving (6)
calories 412, protein 12 g,
fat 32 g, sodium 585 mg,
carbohydrates 13 g,
potassium 231 mg

TIME

1 hour preparation
40 minutes cooking

INGREDIENTS

½ cup plus 1 tablespoon butter
1 small onion, minced
1 clove garlic, peeled and minced
1 can (7¾ ounces) pink salmon or 8
   ounces cooked crab meat, bones
   and skin removed and slightly
   shredded
¾ cup dry white wine
8 ounces cream cheese, softened
¼ to ½ teaspoon salt

2 teaspoons Worcestershire sauce
Hot pepper sauce
3 ounces phyllo dough
Toasted sliced almonds

Preheat oven to 350 degrees. Melt 1 tablespoon of butter in a sauté pan. Sauté onion until soft. Add garlic and sauté 1 minute. Add salmon or crab meat and wine and simmer until all liquid has evaporated. Cool slightly. Melt remaining butter and set aside. Combine salmon or crab meat mixture with cream cheese, salt, Worcestershire, and enough hot pepper sauce to make mixture spicy.

On damp kitchen towel, place 2 sheets of phyllo. Sprinkle liberally with butter. Add 2 more sheets. Sprinkle with butter. Continue in this manner until 8 sheets are used. Place filling along one edge of dough, leaving about 3 inches of space on either side ①. Lift towel slightly and allow dough to roll 2 full turns ②. Tuck sides of dough toward center and continue rolling until strudel is shaped something like a large cigar ③. Roll onto greased jellyroll pan, making sure dough end is on the bottom. Cut a few slits in the top of strudel to allow steam to escape. Sprinkle liberally with butter and bake for 40 minutes or until golden. If dough is not golden after 40 minutes, turn oven heat to broil and place under broiler for a few seconds until strudel is golden. Watch carefully; it will brown very quickly. Sprinkle with a few toasted sliced almonds before serving. Serve hot.

SIRLOIN TERIYAKI

YIELD

8 to 12 servings

Per serving (8)
calories 367, protein 20 g,
fat 26 g, sodium 2024 mg,
carbohydrates 10 g,
potassium 351 mg

TIME

15 minutes preparation
2 hours marinating
3 to 8 minutes cooking

INGREDIENTS

2 pounds boneless sirloin
¾ cup pineapple juice
¾ cup soy sauce
2 tablespoons honey
1 clove garlic, peeled and mashed
Lots of fresh-cracked black pepper
    (about 1 teaspoon or to taste)

Cut steak into ¼-inch-thick slices ①. Combine pineapple juice, soy sauce, honey, garlic, and pepper. Add sirloin ② and marinate at least 2 hours in the refrigerator.

Soak bamboo skewers in cold water for 30 minutes. Thread beef slices onto skewers ③ and broil (either over hot coals or in stove broiler) until beef is cooked to desired doneness. Return beef to marinade and serve either warm or tepid.

ROASTED RED PEPPERS AND OLIVES IN FRESH LIME JUICE

YIELD

4 to 6 servings

Per serving (4)
calories 60, protein 1 g,
fat 3 g, sodium 255 mg,
carbohydrates 8 g,
potassium 230 mg

TIME

10 minutes preparation
15 minutes cooking

INGREDIENTS

4 red bell peppers
1 can (3¼ ounces) pitted black olives,
    drained
3 tablespoons lime juice
¼ teaspoon salt
1 large clove garlic, peeled and
    minced

Preheat broiler. Place peppers in broiler, turning frequently, until they are charred on all sides ①. Remove from oven and cool.

Slice olives. In serving bowl, combine lime juice, salt, and garlic. Add olives.

When peppers are cool enough to handle, peel ②, seed, and slice into strips ③. Add strips to olive/lime mixture. Stir to combine. Serve cold or tepid.

YIELD

10 servings (about 30)

Per serving (fritters only)
calories 165, protein 3 g,
fat 10 g, sodium 230 mg,
carbohydrates 15 g,
potassium 80 mg

TIME

30 minutes preparation
20 minutes cooking

INGREDIENTS

Oil for deep-frying
½ cup heavy cream
2 eggs, beaten
1 cup all-purpose flour
½ teaspoon salt
1½ teaspoons baking powder
1½ teaspoons sugar
1 can (7 ounces) corn, drained
1 small green pepper, seeded and
   diced

1 jar or can (2 ounces) pimientos,
   drained and minced

GINGER SYRUP

3 tablespoons grated or minced fresh
   gingerroot
3 tablespoons dry white wine
¾ cup maple syrup

Start ginger syrup. Simmer ginger and wine together until the wine evaporates. Add syrup and simmer 20 minutes. When syrup is finished, strain, pressing out as much liquid as possible from the ginger. Discard ginger. You should have about ¾ cup.

While syrup cooks, prepare the fritters. Preheat 1 inch of vegetable oil in a heavy-bottomed pan to 350 degrees.

Pour cream into bowl. Add eggs and whisk to blend. Sift together flour, salt, baking powder, and sugar. Stir into cream mixture just to moisten ①; don't beat. Stir in vegetables. Drop batter by tablespoonfuls into hot oil ②. Don't crowd. Fry until golden on bottom, about 2 minutes. Turn and fry top side ③. Remove and drain on paper towels. Place on serving platter with bowl of ginger syrup. Serve hot.

NOTE The composition of the ginger syrup is estimated at 1 tablespoon per serving; calories 39, sodium 1 mg, carbohydrates 9 g, potassium 31 mg.

7

YIELD

6 servings
(12 to 14 drumettes)

Per serving
calories 249, protein 17 g,
fat 11 g, sodium 107 mg,
carbohydrates 16 g,
potassium 156 mg

TIME

25 minutes preparation
20 minutes cooking

INGREDIENTS

2 pounds chicken wings
Oil for deep-frying
1 whole egg
1 tablespoon water
1 cup all-purpose flour
Salt and cayenne
Ginger Syrup (Recipe 6)

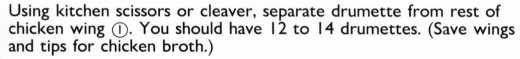

Using kitchen scissors or cleaver, separate drumette from rest of chicken wing ①. You should have 12 to 14 drumettes. (Save wings and tips for chicken broth.)

Preheat 1 inch of oil in heavy-bottomed pan to between 350 and 375 degrees.

Beat together egg and water. Mix flour with salt and cayenne to taste on large platter. Dip drumettes into egg, then into flour ②, turning to coat all sides.

Place drumettes in oil; don't crowd. Fry on both sides until golden, about 4 minutes per side ③. Drain on paper towels. Arrange on platter with bowl of ginger syrup in the center for dipping. Serve hot or tepid.

YIELD

6 to 8 servings
(about 1 cup)

Per serving (6)
calories 249, protein 14 g,
fat 20 g, sodium 357 mg,
carbohydrates 2 g,
potassium 57 mg

TIME

10 minutes preparation
5 minutes cooking

INGREDIENTS

1 tablespoon butter
1 large clove garlic, peeled and
   minced
2 cups grated aged cheddar cheese
1 cup grated monterey jack cheese
3 tablespoons beer
½ teaspoon Worcestershire sauce
3 seeded and chopped green chilies
   (or to taste)
Hot pepper sauce
Corn tortillas or corn chips

In a nonstick saucepan, melt butter and sauté garlic until soft ①. Do not allow to brown or garlic will take on a bitter taste. Add cheeses and cook, stirring ②, over medium heat until cheeses are melted. Stir in remaining ingredients ③, adding pepper sauce until cheese has a slightly spicy taste.

Serve dip hot with deep-fried corn tortillas or crispy corn chips. This dip can be made in advance and reheated over a low flame, stirring constantly.

NOTE Unless it is to be consumed immediately, it is best to keep this hot cheese dip warm in a chafing dish over a low heat.

9

YIELD

12 servings
(24 pieces)

Per serving (12)
calories 39, protein 2 g,
fat 3 g, sodium 463 mg,
carbohydrates .5 g,
potassium 40 mg

TIME

30 minutes preparation
1 hour chilling

INGREDIENTS

1 tablespoon minced fresh parsley
2 teaspoons well-drained prepared
    white horseradish
3 ounces cream cheese
6 pieces (2 by 4 inches) smoked
    salmon
6 asparagus spears, each 4 inches
    long, cooked

Cream together parsley, horseradish, and cream cheese.

Spread about 1 tablespoon of the cream cheese mixture over each salmon strip ①. Place asparagus over cream cheese on the long side ②. Fold or roll salmon over to enclose asparagus ③. Chill 1 hour.

Before serving, cut each strip into 4 1-inch pieces. Serve cold, with toothpicks.

NOTE If desired, place 3 salmon rolls on a lettuce-lined plate and serve as first course. (Makes 2 servings as a first course.)

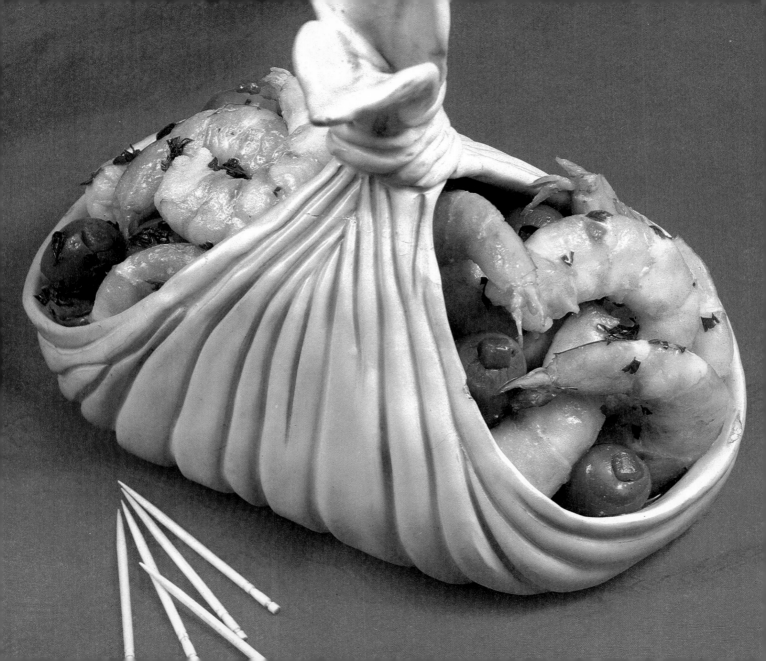

YIELD

8 servings

Per serving
calories 130, protein 10 g,
fat 8 g, sodium 432 mg,
carbohydrates 1 g,
potassium 146 mg

TIME

20 minutes preparation
1 hour chilling

INGREDIENTS

1 pound shelled, deveined extra-large
   shrimp (fresh or frozen)
2 tablespoons minced fresh parsley
   (optional)
4 tablespoons lemon juice
4 tablespoons olive oil
3 tablespoons strong prepared
   mustard (such as Creole style or
   green peppercorn)
1 teaspoon hot pepper sauce

Salt and black pepper
½ cup small pimiento-stuffed green
   olives or 2 tablespoons capers

Place shrimp in pot of boiling, salted water to cover and cook just until shrimp turn pink ①—2 to 6 minutes depending on whether shrimp are fresh or frozen. Drain shrimp.

In a bowl, whisk together parsley, lemon juice, olive oil, mustard, hot pepper sauce, and salt and pepper to taste ②. Add shrimp and olives ③. Chill 1 hour. Pour into serving bowl and serve with toothpicks. Serve cold.

WHOLE-WHEAT PRETZELS

YIELD

12 servings
(about 2 dozen)

Per serving
calories 156, protein 5 g,
fat 1 g, sodium 1215 mg,
carbohydrates 31 g,
potassium 118 mg

TIME

45 minutes preparation
25 minutes cooking

INGREDIENTS

1 package active dry yeast
1 1/2 teaspoons sugar
1 1/2 cups very warm water
3/4 teaspoon salt
2 cups all-purpose flour
2 cups whole-wheat flour
1 tablespoon caraway seeds
1 whole egg
Coarse salt

Preheat oven to 400 degrees.

Place yeast and sugar in large bowl. Add water, stir, and set aside for 5 minutes for yeast to dissolve. Stir in salt and flours. Knead in caraway seeds. Turn out onto lightly floured board and knead 8 to 10 minutes.

Cover a cookie sheet with foil and grease it lightly.

Break off dough by heaping tablespoonfuls, about the size of a lime ①. Roll each into a 10-inch length ②. Bring the ends of the dough to the center to form a B ③. Pinch ends to seal. Place on cookie sheet. Beat egg and brush on pretzels. Sprinkle with coarse salt. Bake for 20 to 25 minutes or until light brown. Serve warm, tepid, or cold.

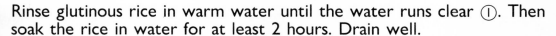
YIELD

12 servings
(about 40 pearl balls)

Per serving
calories 160, protein 7 g,
fat 8 g, sodium 415 mg,
carbohydrates 14 g,
potassium 140 mg

TIME

25 minutes preparation
2 hours soaking
45 minutes cooking

INGREDIENTS

1 cup glutinous (sweet) rice
1 pound ground pork
6 water chestnuts, finely chopped
1 tablespoon minced fresh gingerroot
1 scallion, both white and green parts
   minced
2 tablespoons soy sauce
1 teaspoon sesame or corn oil
1 teaspoon salt
1/2 teaspoon sugar
1/4 teaspoon black pepper
1 tablespoon cornstarch

Rinse glutinous rice in warm water until the water runs clear ①. Then soak the rice in water for at least 2 hours. Drain well.

Combine remaining ingredients in a bowl. Make balls about 1 inch in diameter. Roll balls in rice until evenly coated ②.

Oil a steamer and place it over simmering water. Add balls ③, cover, and steam for 45 minutes. Double-check every 15 minutes to make sure water has not boiled away. The pearl balls are cooked when the centers are no longer pink. (Cut one open to check.) Serve hot.

NOTE Pearl balls can be made the night before, placed in greased pan, covered tightly with plastic wrap, and refrigerated until ready to steam. Steaming will take about 10 minutes longer.

Glutinous rice is available in oriental food markets.

CHERRY TOMATOES WITH BASIL MAYONNAISE

YIELD

8 to 12 servings

Per serving (8)
calories 271, protein 1 g,
fat 29 g, sodium 180 mg,
carbohydrates 1 g,
potassium 81 mg

TIME

20 minutes preparation

INGREDIENTS

1 pint cherry tomatoes
Salt
1/3 cup firmly packed fresh basil leaves
1 whole egg, at room temperature
1 egg yolk, at room temperature
1/4 to 1/2 teaspoon salt
1 tablespoon lemon juice
1/2 cup corn oil
1/2 cup olive oil

Cut tomatoes in half and sprinkle very lightly with salt. Invert and allow to drain ① while you make the mayonnaise.

In a blender or food processor, whirl basil leaves until a paste ②. Add egg, egg yolk, salt, and lemon juice and blend until fluffy (about 30 seconds). With machine running, add oils in a very slow ③, thin stream until all oil is added. This should take several minutes.

Place tomatoes right side up on a serving plate lined with greens. Top each with a generous 1/2 teaspoon of basil mayonnaise. Serve cold.

NOTE Leftover basil mayonnaise is delicious served with cold poached fish or artichokes.

YIELD

6 servings
(12 tartlets)

Per serving
calories 347, protein 10 g,
fat 27 g, sodium 507 mg,
carbohydrates 14 g,
potassium 100 mg

TIME

50 minutes preparation
25 minutes cooking

INGREDIENTS

Pastry for 1 9-inch pie crust (use
    favorite recipe)
6 tablespoons blue cheese, crumbled
2 whole eggs
½ cup heavy cream
¼ cup milk
4 ounces mild cheese (monterey jack
    or brick), grated
¼ teaspoon ground nutmeg
¼ teaspoon salt

Preheat oven to 400 degrees.

Roll out pastry on floured board, to form a 12-inch circle. Using a 3-inch cutter, cut rounds of dough. By reworking dough scraps there should be 12 rounds. Grease the back of a 12-cup muffin pan. Fit rounds onto pan and part way up sides of cups, pressing lightly to seal ①. Bake for 10 minutes. If pastry has puffed up, press down lightly. Set aside to cool.

Reduce oven temperature to 350 degrees.

Remove pastry shells from backs of muffin pan and place upright on cookie sheet. Place ½ tablespoon of blue cheese in bottom of each shell ②. Combine eggs, cream, milk, grated cheese, nutmeg, and salt. Divide mixture among shells, pouring almost to the top ③. Don't overfill, as cheese mixture will rise during baking. There may be some leftover filling. Place filled shells in oven and bake for 15 minutes or until lightly browned and firm. Serve hot or tepid.

CHICKEN LIVER MOUSSE

YIELD

8 servings (2 cups)

Per serving
calories 175, protein 11 g,
fat 11 g, sodium 224 mg,
carbohydrates 3 g,
potassium 126 mg

TIME

1 hour preparation
1 hour chilling

INGREDIENTS

3 tablespoons butter
4 tablespoons minced onion
1 pound chicken livers, trimmed of fat
2 tablespoons plum or pear brandy,
   warmed
Salt to taste
¼ teaspoon ground allspice
1 teaspoon quatre epice
½ cup heavy cream
2 tablespoons minced fresh parsley

Melt butter in large skillet. Add onion and sauté 5 minutes, until tender. Add chicken livers, half at a time, turning to brown all sides (livers should remain pink inside) ①. Remove livers and onion. Pour off fat.

Return onion and livers to skillet. Turn heat to very low. Add brandy and flame ②. When flames die, remove skillet from heat and allow to cool 10 minutes.

Pour livers, onions, and pan juices into blender or food processor fitted with steel blade. Add salt, allspice, and *quatre epice* and process to a purée. Place strainer over medium-size bowl. Press livers through strainer a few tablespoons at a time ③. Discard fibers that don't go through (this step isn't essential, but results in a finer mousse).

Whip cream until stiff. Fold in liver purée and then place in 2½- to 3-cup crock. Top with parsley and chill at least 1 hour before serving. Don't make more than one day in advance. Serve cold.

NOTE Quatre epice is a French term for a mixture of ground spices, usually pepper, nutmeg, cloves, and cinnamon or ginger; pepper predominates. This is available commercially or can be made according to taste at home.

YIELD

6 to 8 servings
(20 wontons)

Per serving (6)
calories 269, protein 6 g,
fat 19 g, sodium 124 mg,
carbohydrates 16 g,
potassium 91 mg

TIME

15 minutes preparation
10 minutes cooking

INGREDIENTS

Oil for deep-frying
1 package (8 ounces) cream cheese
20 wonton wrappers
5 teaspoons chopped scallions, both
    white and green parts
Curry powder
1 whole egg, beaten
Soy sauce or sweet and sour sauce
    for dipping

Heat oil to 350 degrees.

Divide cream cheese into 20 equal parts. Place a cream cheese cube on top of each wonton wrapper. Top each with about ¼ teaspoon scallion and a dash or 2 of curry powder ①. Brush 2 adjacent sides of each wrapper with beaten egg and fold wrapper over to seal into a triangular shape ②.

Deep-fry wontons in hot oil until golden ③. Drain on paper towel. Serve hot with a bowl of soy sauce or commercially made sweet and sour sauce on the side.

YIELD

6 to 8 servings

Per serving (6)
calories 358, protein 11 g,
fat 18 g, sodium 306 mg,
carbohydrates 38 g,
potassium 214 mg

TIME

30 minutes preparation

INGREDIENTS

4 tablespoons peanut butter, either
   smooth or crunchy
1 tablespoon soy sauce
3 tablespoons brown sugar
1/4 to 1/2 teaspoon cayenne
5 tablespoons sesame or corn oil
8 ounces thin whole-wheat pasta,
   cooked and hot
1/2 cup shelled peas, cooked
2 scallions, both white and green
   parts chopped

1 medium unpeeled and sliced
   cucumber
3 tablespoons chopped peanuts
1 to 2 tablespoons chopped fresh
   coriander (cilantro)

In a bowl, combine peanut butter, soy sauce, brown sugar, cayenne, and 1 tablespoon sesame or corn oil ①.

Toss cooked, hot pasta with remaining 4 tablespoons oil ②. Immediately add peanut sauce and toss until sauce is melted and thoroughly distributed ③. Fold in peas and scallions.

Arrange sliced cucumber around perimeter of serving dish. Mound pasta onto plate. Sprinkle pasta with chopped peanuts and coriander to taste. Serve tepid.

YIELD

12 servings (40 to 50)

Per serving
calories 230, protein 5 g,
fat 20 g, sodium 318 mg,
carbohydrates 8 g,
potassium 108 mg

TIME

45 minutes preparation
1 hour chilling

INGREDIENTS

4 ounces carp-roe caviar (see note)
2 tablespoons cold water
1 cup fresh bread crumbs
4 tablespoons lemon juice
1 cup olive oil
1/4 cup minced onion
1 small clove garlic, peeled and
   minced
1 tablespoon minced fresh dill
   (or 1 teaspoon dried)
Salt and black pepper to taste
40 to 50 fresh snow peas

In blender or food processor fitted with steel blade, place carp-roe caviar and cold water. Blend briefly. Add bread crumbs and lemon juice and blend briefly again. Trickle in oil as you would for making mayonnaise ①. When mixture is thick and oil is used, add onion, garlic, and dill and blend until smooth. Season very lightly with salt, if necessary, and add pepper to taste. Set aside.

Steam snow peas about 3 minutes, until they puff up and turn bright green (they will deflate again). When cool enough to handle, trim off stem end and strings ②. This will open peas. Fill each pea with 1/2 to 1 tablespoon taramosalata, depending on the size of the pea. This can be done by hand or with a pastry tube ③. Chill 1 hour. Serve cold.

NOTE *Carp-roe caviar is available in jars in Greek food stores and is called* tarama. *If unavailable, substitute 4 ounces of the cheapest and strongest-flavored red caviar.*

YIELD

10 servings
(32 cheese sticks)

Per serving
calories 127, protein 5 g,
fat 8 g, sodium 262 mg,
carbohydrates 7 g,
potassium 23 mg

TIME

45 minutes preparation
15 minutes cooking

INGREDIENTS

4 tablespoons butter
4 ounces parmesan cheese, grated
1 to 1½ teaspoons hot pepper sauce
¾ cup all-purpose flour

Preheat oven to 375 degrees.

Cream butter in electric mixer or by hand. Gradually add cheese. Add hot pepper sauce. Then gradually add flour. If necessary, add cold water by the teaspoon to form dough that will stick together ①.

Divide dough in half. Cover with plastic wrap and let rest 15 minutes. Roll out one half at a time to a rectangle 8 by 5 inches. Trim edges ②. Cut in half widthwise to 2 strips 8 inches long and 2½ inches wide. Cut strips into 1-inch sticks along the length (to yield 8 sticks per strip) ③. Place on ungreased cookie sheet. Repeat with remaining dough.

Bake 15 minutes or until sticks are faintly brown. Store in cool, dry place. Serve cold or tepid.

YIELD

6 to 8 servings
(14 sandwiches)

Per serving (6)
calories 178, protein 10 g,
fat 10 g, sodium 283 mg,
carbohydrates 10 g,
potassium 117 mg

TIME

15 minutes preparation

INGREDIENTS

1 can (4½ ounces) deveined broken
   shrimp
3 scallions, both white and green
   parts thinly sliced
3 tablespoons sour cream
4 tablespoons mayonnaise
6 tablespoons finely grated parmesan
   cheese
White pepper to taste
14 slices party rye bread
14 whole cooked and cleaned shrimp
14 tiny sprigs fresh parsley or mint

Drain the canned shrimp ①.

Combine scallions, canned shrimp, sour cream, mayonnaise, cheese, and a dash or two of pepper. Mix by hand until almost smooth ②. Spread each slice of bread with about 1 tablespoon of shrimp mixture ③. Top each with 1 shrimp and a sprig of parsley or mint. Serve cold.

YIELD

12 servings (3 dozen)

Per serving
calories 205, protein 8 g,
fat 18 g, sodium 453 mg,
carbohydrates 1 g,
potassium 122 mg

TIME

25 minutes preparation
1 hour chilling

INGREDIENTS

1 pound ripe brie or camembert
  cheese
About 3 dozen small pimiento-stuffed
  green olives or pitted black olives
1 cup finely chopped pecans

Remove rind from cheese (either discard or save for another recipe) ①.

Pat olives dry. Shape about ½ tablespoon cheese around each olive ②. Place nuts on plate and roll each cheese ball in nuts to coat ③. Chill 1 hour before serving. Serve cold.

22

YIELD

12 servings (1 pound)

Per serving

calories 292, protein 3 g,
fat 26 g, sodium 28 mg,
carbohydrates 13 g,
potassium 240 mg

TIME

15 minutes preparation
1 hour, 15 minutes
   cooking

INGREDIENTS

1 large egg white
1 teaspoon pecan-flavored liqueur or
   rum
1 pound large pecan halves
$\frac{1}{3}$ cup granulated sugar
2 tablespoons brown sugar
$\frac{1}{8}$ teaspoon salt
$\frac{3}{4}$ teaspoon ground cinnamon

Preheat oven to 225 degrees.

Whip egg white in large bowl until frothy ①. Add liqueur. Add nuts and toss ②. Add granulated and brown sugars, salt, and cinnamon and toss well to coat.

Spread mixture on greased cookie sheet ③. Place in oven. Turn nuts every 15 minutes and bake a total of 1 hour and 15 minutes. Store nuts in cool, dry place. Serve cold.

23

YIELD

8 to 12 servings
(about 34 samosas)

Per serving (8)
calories 327, protein 5 g,
fat 23 g, sodium 373 mg,
carbohydrates 23 g,
potassium 110 mg

TIME

30 minutes preparation
25 minutes cooking

INGREDIENTS

⅓ cup chopped onion
1 tablespoon butter
1 tablespoon curry powder
½ teaspoon paprika
¼ teaspoon salt
½ teaspoon ground cinnamon
5 tablespoons heavy cream
½ cup cooked ground lamb or beef,
  or cooked and chopped potato
2 tablespoons raisins

2 tablespoons chopped walnuts
Pastry for 2 9-inch pie crusts (use
  favorite recipe)
1 egg white, beaten

Preheat oven to 350 degrees. Sauté the onion in butter until onion is soft. Add curry powder, paprika, salt, and cinnamon and cook for 30 seconds, stirring constantly. Add cream and cook until it just begins to thicken, stirring constantly ①. Add cooked meat or potatoes, raisins, and walnuts and continue cooking until mixture is almost dry. Let sit for 10 minutes to cool.

Roll out pastry and cut into rounds that are 2½ inches in diameter ②. Place about 1 teaspoon of filling into center of each round and pinch edges of dough together to form half circles ③. Repeat until all filling is used, using a little egg white to help seal shut if necessary. Brush each samosa with egg white and bake for 25 minutes or until golden. Serve hot or tepid.

YIELD

4 servings

Per serving
calories 318, protein 10 g,
fat 24 g, sodium 432 mg,
carbohydrates 15 g,
potassium 125 mg

TIME

20 minutes preparation
20 minutes cooking

INGREDIENTS

2 frozen patty shells (commercially
prepared puff pastry shells),
thawed
1 round (4½ ounces) camembert
cheese, not fully ripened
1 rounded tablespoon apricot or
raspberry jam
2 tablespoons slivered almonds
1 egg, beaten

Preheat oven to 425 degrees.

On lightly floured board, roll each patty shell to a 6-inch circle ①. Place cheese round in center of one circle. Spread with jam and sprinkle nuts on top ②. Cover with second dough round and press edges to seal. Trim off excess. Press edges up and curl into a ring around the cheese ③.

Brush surface with beaten egg. Place on ungreased cookie sheet and bake for 20 minutes or until golden. Cut into quarters and serve warm on individual plates.

NOTE If desired, recipe can be doubled or tripled. It isn't necessary to increase amount of egg.

YIELD

12 servings
(24 triangles)

Per serving
calories 351, protein 17 g,
fat 19 g, sodium 268 mg,
carbohydrates 26 g,
potassium 159 mg

TIME

1 hour, 15 minutes
preparation
20 minutes cooking

INGREDIENTS

1 cup butter, melted
3 eggs, beaten
3 cups chopped cooked boneless
   chicken breast
1/4 teaspoon saffron dissolved in
   1 tablespoon chicken broth
   (if desired, just use the broth)
1/4 teaspoon ground coriander
1/2 teaspoon ground nutmeg
3/4 teaspoon ground gingerroot

1 1/2 teaspoons ground cinnamon
3 tablespoons sugar
1/4 cup light or dark raisins
1/4 cup pine nuts
Salt and freshly ground black pepper
16 sheets phyllo dough

Place 2 tablespoons melted butter in top of double boiler. Add beaten eggs and cook, stirring often, until mixture resembles slightly underdone scrambled eggs. Stir in chicken. Add saffron mixture, along with coriander, nutmeg, ginger, 1 teaspoon cinnamon, 1 tablespoon sugar, raisins, pine nuts, and salt and pepper to taste. Mix well.

Preheat oven to 350 degrees.

Lay 2 sheets of phyllo dough, one on top of the other, on board or cookie sheet (keep remaining 14 covered with slightly damp cloth). Brush generously with melted butter. Cut into 3 vertical strips ①. Place a heaping tablespoon of the chicken mixture in corner of one strip and fold into triangle, then continue folding in triangles all the way up the strip ②. Trim off excess. Press edges of dough in to seal using more butter ③. Place triangle on ungreased cookie sheet.

Repeat making triangles with remaining 2 strips. Then repeat the entire process 7 more times (using 2 sheets of phyllo for each, cutting each into 3 strips). You'll have 24 triangles in all.

Mix together remaining 2 tablespoons sugar and remaining 1/2 teaspoon cinnamon. Brush triangles with remaining butter and sprinkle with sugar-cinnamon mixture. Bake for 20 minutes or until golden brown. Serve hot or tepid.

YIELD

10 servings

Per serving
calories 146, protein 11 g,
fat 6 g, sodium 160 mg,
carbohydrates 4 g,
potassium 192 mg

TIME

1 hour preparation
30 minutes cooking

INGREDIENTS

5 cups water
1 cup dry vermouth
4 or 5 cracked black peppercorns
2 bay leaves
2 chicken breasts, cut in half
3 tablespoons mayonnaise
1 tablespoon minced fresh chives
³/₄ teaspoon curry powder
¹/₂ teaspoon salt
¹/₄ teaspoon black pepper
1 papaya

Place water and vermouth in a 3-quart saucepan along with the cracked peppercorns and bay leaves. Bring to boil, then add chicken. Reduce heat and simmer 30 minutes or until chicken is done. Remove chicken from broth and set aside to cool.

Remove chicken skin and bones ①. Cut chicken into 1-inch cubes ②.

Combine mayonnaise, chives, curry powder, salt, and pepper. Add chicken and toss gently, but well.

Peel, halve, and seed papaya ③. Cut each half into 1-inch cubes. Using wooden skewers, start each kabob with papaya chunk and alternate papaya and chicken cubes. Serve cold.

27

YIELD

6 servings

Per serving
calories 220, protein 4 g,
fat 14 g, sodium 219 mg,
carbohydrates 18 g,
potassium 205 mg

TIME

35 minutes preparation
10 minutes cooking

INGREDIENTS

1 package (7 ounces) mild goat
   cheese, or 5 ounces goat cheese
   plus 2 ounces softened cream
   cheese
1 tablespoon minced chives
1 tablespoon beaten egg
Coarsely ground black pepper
12 large grape leaves
Olive oil

Preheat oven to 350 degrees.

Cream together cheese, chives, egg, and pepper to taste.

Wash grape leaves and pat dry. Remove stems ①. Working with one leaf at a time, place 1 rounded tablespoon of the cheese mixture at stem end of each leaf ②. Roll up tightly, tucking ends in to form a cigar shape. Place rolls, open end down, on a greased baking sheet ③. Brush with olive oil. Bake for 10 minutes. Serve hot or tepid.

NOTE *Grape leaves are available in jars in Greek or Middle Eastern food stores.*

YIELD

5 to 6 servings

Per serving (5)
calories 276, protein 5 g,
fat 13 g, sodium 242 mg,
carbohydrates 36 g,
potassium 458 mg

TIME

30 minutes preparation
1 hour chilling

INGREDIENTS

1 cup cracked wheat (bulgur)
1 cup boiling water
4 to 5 tablespoons olive oil
4 tablespoons lemon juice
½ teaspoon salt
½ cup minced fresh parsley
1 clove garlic, peeled and minced
    (optional)
2 tablespoons minced scallion, green
    part only

4 tablespoons minced fresh mint
1 fresh tomato, cored and diced
Coarsely ground black pepper
10 red cabbage leaves

Place cracked wheat in medium-size heatproof bowl. Add boiling water ① and set aside 15 minutes. Add olive oil, lemon juice, salt, parsley, garlic, scallion, mint, tomato, and pepper to taste ②. Chill 1 hour for flavors to blend.

Spoon ½ cup of the cracked wheat mixture into the center of each cabbage leaf ③. Arrange attractively on serving platter to resemble cups. Serve as part of a buffet table or first course for sit-down dinner. Serve cold or tepid.

TOMATO SALSA WITH ORANGE

YIELD

10 to 12 servings
(about 2¾ cups)

Per serving (10)
calories 18, protein .7 g,
fat .1 g, sodium 167 mg,
carbohydrates 4 g,
potassium 121 mg

TIME

15 minutes preparation
2 hours chilling

INGREDIENTS

2 scallions, both white and green
    parts sliced
¼ cup chopped onion
2 tablespoons minced fresh coriander
    (cilantro)
2 serrano or jalapeno chilies (or to
    taste), finely minced
½ teaspoon salt
½ teaspoon sugar
Grated peel of 1 orange

1 can (16 ounces) tomatoes, chopped
    with juice reserved
Hot pepper sauce
Corn tortillas or corn chips

Combine all ingredients except hot pepper sauce, including juice from tomatoes. Add hot pepper sauce to taste. Chill for at least 2 hours. Serve as a dip with deep-fried corn tortillas or corn chips. Serve cold.

NOTE Nutritional analysis does not include tortilla.

HUNGARIAN CHEESE SPREAD

YIELD

8 to 10 servings
(about 1¼ cups)

Per serving (8)
calories 157, protein 1 g,
fat 16 g, sodium 212 mg,
carbohydrates 1 g,
potassium 48 mg

TIME

10 minutes preparation
1 hour chilling

INGREDIENTS

3 ounces cream cheese, softened
¼ cup sour cream
½ cup butter, softened
2 tablespoons minced onion
2 teaspoons caraway seeds
1½ teaspoons paprika
½ teaspoon prepared mustard
2 heaping tablespoons chopped
    pimiento-stuffed green olives

With an electric mixer, blender, or food processor, whip together cream cheese, sour cream, butter, onion, caraway seeds, paprika, and mustard. By hand, stir in olives. Refrigerate at least 1 hour or until using.

Remove spread from refrigerator at least 30 minutes before serving, and serve with crackers, toast points, or pumpernickel bread.

FETA AND DILL DIP

YIELD

8 to 10 servings
(about 1 cup)

Per serving (8)
calories 72, protein 2 g,
fat 6 g, sodium 196 mg,
carbohydrates 1 g,
potassium 52 mg

TIME

10 minutes preparation

INGREDIENTS

1 cup crumbled feta cheese
2 tablespoons dill weed (dried)
1/2 cup sour cream

Mix all ingredients in a blender or food processor. Serve cold with fresh vegetables.

MUSHROOMS MARINATED IN RED WINE

YIELD

4 to 6 servings

Per serving (4)
calories 217, protein 1 g,
fat 14 g, sodium 18 mg,
carbohydrates 21 g,
potassium 281 mg

TIME

15 minutes preparation
24 hours marinating

INGREDIENTS

1/3 cup sugar
2 tablespoons dry red wine
1 cup red wine vinegar
1/4 cup corn or vegetable oil
8 ounces fresh whole mushrooms,
    cleaned

Combine sugar, red wine, red wine vinegar, and oil. Add mushrooms and marinate in refrigerator for 24 hours. Stir occasionally. Serve cold.

INDEX

The following numbers refer to the recipe numbers, not page numbers.